GOD ANSWERS PRAYER

for girls

GOD ANSWERS PRAYER

PRAYER

for girls

IRENE HOWAT

CF4·K

10 9 8 7 6 5 4 3 2 1
© Copyright 2013 Christian Focus Publications
ISBN: 978-1-78191-151-8

Published by Christian Focus Publications,
Geanies House, Fearn, Tain, Ross-shire,
IV20 1TW, Scotland, U.K.
www.christianfocus.com
E-mail: info@christianfocus.com

Cover design by Daniel van Straaten
Cover illustration by Neil Reed

Character illustration by Brent Donahoe
Printed and bound by Bell and Bain, Glasgow

FOR
EILIDH CATHERINE
STEWART

CONTENTS

THE WOMAN WHO WANTED A BABY

About a thousand years before Jesus was born, a man called Elkanah was married to two wives, one was called Hannah and the other Peninnah. Peninnah had children, but Hannah had none and that made her sad. When she watched Peninnah cuddling her babies and playing with her toddlers she wished she had a baby of her own to cuddle, she wished she had a toddler to play with. But she didn't.

As if having no children wasn't bad enough, poor Hannah had to put up with Peninnah herself. It was difficult to share a husband, but Peninnah made it more difficult because she was very unkind.

'Elkanah loves me more than he loves you because I had his children,' she would boast to Hannah.

This went on and on and on. Every year Elkanah went with his wives to worship God at a place called Shiloh. That should have been a happy time for

Hannah because she believed in God and worshipped him. But it wasn't a happy time at all because Peninnah could be particularly nasty on special occasions. In fact, she was so nasty that Hannah ended up in tears and unable to eat her dinner.

'Hannah, why are you weeping?' Elkanah asked. 'Why don't you eat your dinner?' And when Hannah explained what was wrong, he said, 'Don't I mean more to you than ten sons?'

The family lived at a time when it was important to have children, especially sons. Elkanah loved Hannah so much that he wanted her to be happy even if she never had a child.

One day, when they were at Shiloh, Hannah went on her own to pray to God about the problem. She was so upset that the tears ran down her face as she prayed. This is what she said:

> 'O Lord Almighty, if you will only look upon your servant's misery and remember me, and not forget your servant, but give her a son, then I will give him to the Lord for all the days of his life, and no razor will ever be used on his head.'

The priest at Shiloh was called Eli and he saw Hannah. He watched her carefully. She was so distressed that while she prayed silently to the Lord her lips moved as though she was speaking aloud. Eli was not happy. She was behaving so oddly he was sure she must be drunk!

'Get rid of your wine,' Eli said.

Hannah looked at the priest. 'Not so, my Lord,' she explained. 'I am deeply troubled. I have not been drinking wine or beer; I was pouring out my soul to the Lord.'

Eli listened carefully.

'Do not take your servant for a wicked woman,' Hannah begged. 'I have been praying out of great anguish and grief.'

The priest didn't ask Hannah what was making her so sad but he spoke kindly to her. 'Go in peace,' he said, 'and may the God of Israel grant you what you have asked of him.'

Hannah stopped crying, joined the others and ate her meal. She had prayed to God and she believed that he would answer.

The next day Elkanah and his family worshipped God and then went back to Ramah. The Lord heard Hannah's prayers and a little later she realised that she was going to have a baby. How happy she must have been! There is a Hebrew word that means 'heard of God' and it sounds a bit like the name Samuel. When he was born Hannah called her baby Samuel. God had heard her prayer and answered her.

You would think that Hannah would have been a very over-protective mother but that wasn't the case. She meant the words she prayed when she said,

'If you will only look upon your servant's misery and remember me, and not forget your servant, but give her a son, then I will give him to the Lord for all the days of his life.'

When Samuel was still quite young, he went with his parents to Shiloh to see Eli the priest.

'I am the woman who stood here beside you praying to the Lord,' she reminded Eli. 'I prayed for this child, and the Lord has granted me what I asked of him. So now for his whole life he shall be given over to the Lord.'

When Hannah and Elkanah went home to Ramah, they left young Samuel there to serve God by helping the old priest.

Hannah didn't forget her little boy. Each year she made him a robe and took it with her when the family went to Shiloh. Over the years Hannah had exciting news for her son because God gave her another three sons and two daughters. Samuel was a big brother to five!

We don't know how long Hannah lived and when she died but we know, for it is told in the Bible, that while he was still a boy Samuel was called to serve the Lord in a special way. For many years he was the most important prophet in the land, leading and guiding God's people. When the time came for Israel to have a king, Samuel was led by God to choose David to be the greatest king the Jewish people ever had.

When Hannah prayed asking God for a baby, she made a promise at the same time. We sometimes do that too. Like Hannah, we must be careful to keep the promises we make to God. He keeps all the promises he makes to us. You'll find them in the Bible.

ANNA'S LONG WAIT

When Anna was a young woman she married and lived with her husband for just seven years before he died. We don't know if she had any children, but she was looking forward to the birth of a very special child. You see, Anna was a member of the Jewish race. Her father's name was Phanuel, and he belonged to the tribe of Asher. So Anna could trace her family tree in the Old Testament!

Anna's Bible was the Old Testament and she knew her Bible. She knew that God had made everything in just seven days. She would have known about God rescuing his people from slavery in Egypt and taking them safely to the Promised Land. Anna knew the Ten Commandments. And she most certainly knew the Good News.

God gave one of the Old Testament prophets the Good News and he wrote it down for all Jewish people as a promise. Anna would have known these words.

'For to us a child is born, to us a son is given, and the government shall be on his shoulders. And he will be called Wonderful Counsellor, Mighty God, Everlasting Father, Prince of Peace.'

The prophet's name was Isaiah and he lived hundreds of years before Anna was born. God didn't say when he was going to send this special child. He expected his people to be patient and to wait for his coming. Anna believed God's promise and she did what he wanted her to do; the young widow in her twenties waited patiently for the coming of the Messiah.

Jewish people had a special place where they went to worship God. It was called a temple. The first temple was built hundreds of years before Anna by King Solomon. As Anna moved through her thirties she spent all her time in the temple, waiting patiently and praying for the coming of the Messiah.

God even told Isaiah a little about the Messiah's mother and it was written in the Old Testament. Anna would have known the words.

'Therefore the Lord himself will give you a sign. The virgin will be with child and will give birth to a son, and will call him Immanuel.'

It was as though God was telling his people little by little what was going to happen so that they could look forward with excitement. And what God told Isaiah was truly exciting for 'Immanuel' means 'God with us'. So they were being told that the Messiah would be born to a young woman and that he would be 'God with us'. The Messiah was going to be God himself! In her forties and fifties Anna spent all her time in the temple, waiting and praying for the coming of the Messiah who was God himself!

Jewish people believed God's promise and waited for the Messiah. Those who knew their Bibles found other clues about his coming. God spoke to another prophet; his name was Micah. This is what he told him.

'But you, Bethlehem, though you are small among the clans of Judah, out of you will come for me one who will be ruler over Israel …'

Not only did God tell his people that he was going to send a Messiah; he even told them the name of the town in which he'd be born! Anna believed God's promise; in her sixties she waited patiently and prayed for the coming of the Messiah.

Anna knew that in the Old Testament praying and fasting went together. Fasting means doing without food. People sometimes went without food for a day or two at a time, or ate only one meal a day. Occasionally people fasted for much longer than that though they still drank plenty of water. Anna knew that she should fast as well as pray. In her seventies, Anna was still in the temple every day – and every night – waiting, praying and fasting for the coming of the Messiah who was God himself.

Although Anna knew exactly who she was waiting for, many at that time were very mixed up. Their country had been taken over by the Romans and they were being ruled by Caesar, the Roman Emperor, instead of their own king. They didn't like that one little bit. Roman soldiers marched the streets. Roman laws had to be kept. Worst of all Roman taxes had to be paid. What people wanted was a mighty, powerful Jewish leader who would raise up an army and chase the Romans out of their country. Many decided that the One for whom they were waiting would be a warrior. But Anna knew better; in her eighties she prayed and fasted as she waited for the Messiah who would be God himself.

Anna was eighty-four and she was in the temple one day as usual. Nothing was different. She was still praying, still fasting, still waiting patiently. Then a couple came to the temple, a young woman and an older man. The young woman was carrying their baby son. Anna knew! She knew immediately. The waiting was over! The promised baby had been born! The Messiah who was God himself was lying there in the arms of his young mother! Anna was so excited, so thrilled! All the years of waiting had been worth it – she had seen the Messiah with her very own old eyes! People round about realised that something was going on. Anna was usually quietly praying and today the old woman was almost dancing with excitement. Her old eyes shone like bright stars.

'The Messiah has come!' she told everyone who passed.

'He's here!' Anna said, pointing at the baby.

'Look! Here's the One we've been waiting for!'

Some people smiled as they sometimes do at old people. Others might have been more interested. No doubt most just walked past.

'What's his name?' Anna must have asked. Who wouldn't?

'His name's Jesus,' she was told.

And Anna would have known what the name Jesus meant. It meant Saviour, for Jesus would save his people from their sins. And dear old Anna knew it.

Sometimes God expects us to wait for a long time for an answer to our prayers. Anna waited until she was eighty-four years old. Perhaps one reason he does that is to teach us patience.

FOR US!

When we love someone we want to do the best we can for them. Jesus loves us more than words can tell. I want to tell you about two absolutely wonderful and loving prayers that Jesus prayed, and one that he's still praying.

About 2,000 years ago, when Jesus was on earth, he prayed for twenty-first century Christians! It was the night before he was crucified. He had a meal with his friends and, because he knew this was the last time they would be together before he died, Jesus made it a special occasion. He explained what was going to happen to him and to them. Then Jesus changed from talking to his friends to talking to his Father in heaven; he began to pray.

First Jesus prayed for himself. After that he prayed for his friends, asking his Father to protect them when he went back home to heaven. Then he prayed these words:

> 'I pray also for those who will believe in me through their message.'

If you believe in the Lord Jesus Christ, that evening, all those centuries ago, Jesus was praying for YOU! This message of God's love was then passed on from one Christian to another, to their sons and daughters, grandsons and granddaughters, friends, servants and slaves.

Churches were started and the message was preached and taught. Missionaries went to foreign countries with the best news in the world. And it has passed on right down the centuries until now, over 2,000 years later, when someone told you about the Saviour. You are reading the message right now!

Would you like to know what else Jesus prayed for you that night? It's right there in the Bible. He prayed,

> 'May they be brought into complete unity to let the world know that you sent me and have loved them even as you have loved me.'

Jesus prayed that Christians would tell other people who are alive today that God loves us so much that he sent his Son to die on the cross so that all who believe in him will be forgiven for their sin and go home to heaven one day. And here's a wonderful thing. Maybe years from now there will be people who become Christians because they learned about

Jesus from someone who heard about him from you.

Now for another wonderful prayer. Before Jesus died on the cross, even though he was suffering so much, he prayed to his Father in heaven. And here is what he said:

'Father, forgive them, for they do not know what they are doing.'

That was quite true. The Jewish leaders and the Roman soldiers really didn't know what they were doing. But let me tell you in just fifty words.

God is so holy that nothing bad can go to heaven to be with him. We are all bad and deserve to be punished. Jesus was punished in our place on the cross so that all who believe in him can be forgiven and go to heaven when they die.

And that's the wonderful message that Jesus wants us to pass on!

Then we come to a third prayer I want to tell you about. You know where Jesus is now, don't you? He's in heaven. And do you ever wonder what Jesus is doing in heaven? Well, we don't know all that he does there, but one thing that the Lord is doing in heaven is praying for us. And he will go on praying for us until we go to be with him for ever and ever and ever and ever.

In heaven Jesus remembers what it was like to be a child. He understands the things that make us happy and the things that make us sad. Jesus remembers what it was like to live in a real family, because he lived in a real family with parents, brothers and sisters. The Lord knows what it is like to feel ill, to be hurt, to be upset. He remembers what it is like when a loved one dies. And when Jesus in heaven prays for you and for me, he knows exactly what our situations are and he understands perfectly. Even when we feel that nobody really understands, Jesus does.

We don't really know very much about heaven, which will make it a great surprise for Christians when we get there. But we do know a little bit. When things go wrong and upset us, it is good to remember where all God's people will go when their lives on earth are over. We know that there will be no pain in heaven, and no sadness or mourning. In fact, the Bible tells us that God will wipe away every tear from our eyes. What a truly glorious place that will be!

From the beginning of the Bible to the end we read about people who prayed to God. Right through history we can find stories of Christians who prayed, some of them girls like you. But the best example of someone who prayed is the Lord Jesus Christ himself. And if God's one and only Son needed to pray, surely you and I need to pray much, much more.

THE WOMAN WHO PRAYED WITH HER HANDS

There was a woman who lived in Jesus' day who for a whole twelve years had an illness that made her bleed all the time. She did what she could to get better but nothing helped. Although the woman spent all her money on doctor's bills, instead of getting better she grew worse and worse. Nothing helped and, after twelve long years, she probably decided that she would have to suffer from her illness for the rest of her life.

Then she heard about Jesus, a wandering preacher who was going round the country preaching and teaching and healing people.

'Would he be able to help me?' she wondered.

She must have been relieved to hear that Jesus didn't charge any money for healing sick people because she had spent all her money on doctors. Having thought the matter through, the woman came up with an amazing plan. She decided that if Jesus was powerful enough to heal her, then she only had to touch his clothes to be healed! It wasn't that she believed in magic, because Jesus is certainly not a magician. God had given her the amazing faith to believe that Jesus was that powerful. What the poor woman didn't know was that she was about to cause Jairus, one of the local church leaders, a very worrying and upsetting time.

Jesus crossed over by boat to the place where the woman lived and a large crowd gathered around him. She was in the crowd and she was determined to put her plan into action, getting as close to Jesus as she could and then reaching out to touch the hem of his clothes. As she pushed her way between the people Jairus, an important man in the town, barged right to the front and fell at Jesus' feet. That was an extraordinary thing to do. Jairus was a ruler in the synagogue and Jesus seemed to be only a wandering preacher, yet the ruler was down on the ground, bowed in front of him!

'My little daughter is dying,' the crowd heard him say. 'Please come and put your hands on her so that she will be healed and live.'

Over the noise of all the people Jesus heard what Jairus said and set out with him for his home. The crowd followed the two men as they walked, and in the crowd was the poor woman, still determined to carry out her plan, still sure that Jesus could heal her. She pushed nearer and nearer until she was near enough.

'If I just touch his clothes, I'll be healed,' she thought, as she stretched as far as she possibly could.

Suddenly she knew without any doubt that she was better. She had been healed! After twelve long years of bleeding the woman knew that she was well again.

The very moment she realised she was healed, Jesus turned round to face her – and to face all the other people who were pushing and shoving around him.

'Who touched my clothes?' Jesus asked.

His eyes would have searched the crowd as he spoke, for he knew that someone had been healed.

'You see the people crowding against you,' his friends answered. 'And yet you ask, "Who touched me?"'

But Jesus knew that someone had touched him in a special and healing way and he looked this way and that in the crowed to see who it was.

Imagine poor Jairus! His daughter was dying and this was his last desperate attempt to save her. And the woman must have known how desperate he was because she would have heard his prayer to Jesus. She was shaking when she fell down at the Lord's feet and poured out her whole story. Jesus said to her, 'Daughter, your faith has healed you. Go in peace and be freed from your suffering.'

Just then a terrible thing happened. Some men came and told Jairus that his little girl had died and that he shouldn't trouble Jesus any more. Imagine how relieved the woman must have been when she heard Jesus telling Jairus not to be afraid; just to believe. What happened after that is truly amazing. Jesus, Jairus and three of Jesus' friends went to the girl's home. By then there was a terrible wailing going on because at that time, and in that part of the world, people gathered to weep and wail after a death. It was their way of showing how sad they were.

Jesus went into that sad home. He told everyone to leave apart from his three friends and the young girl's parents.

'The child is not dead but asleep,' he told them.

The people could see that the girl was dead and they laughed at the Lord! They were right to say she was dead. Jesus told them she was asleep because he was going to bring her back to life again. But they were terribly wrong to laugh at him.

Jesus then went up to the girl, took her hand and spoke to her. 'Talitha koum!' he said. (That means, 'Little girl, I say to you, get up!')

Right away the girl got up and walked around the room! Imagine how her parents felt! They were totally amazed, delighted, thrilled, grateful … and lots more wonderful feelings all at the same time.

'Give her something to eat,' Jesus said.

And no doubt her mum rushed to the kitchen and made the happiest little meal of her life.

This story is really two answered prayer stories. One prayer wasn't said in words because the woman who was healed believed in Jesus but didn't have the courage to ask him to heal her. And the other prayer was said in words when Jairus asked the Lord Jesus to come and put his hands on his daughter so that she would live. God hears the words we say to him and he also hears the deep things in our hearts that we don't know how to put into words.

OOOPS ... RHODA!

Rhoda was a servant girl. One of her jobs was to help look after visitors. Her mistress, whose name was Mary, often had visitors. The house was big and could hold a good number of people. Once there was a special meeting in the house even though it was the middle of the night. The servant girl knew that the visitors were there because they were worried. Sometimes when a lot of people are in a house together there's a great deal of chat and laughter. There was very little chat that night and no laughter at all.

The problem was that the early Christians were in trouble. It wasn't long since Jesus had died and risen again and those who believed in him were full of enthusiasm for telling people about him. But not everyone wanted to know. King Herod had a number of Christians arrested and killed! Those who didn't like what Jesus' friends were saying told King Herod what a splendid idea this was. As he really liked being popular the king decided to have Peter arrested as well.

Everyone knew Peter. That wasn't because he was better than the other Christians, nor was it because he was cleverer or more handsome than his fellow believers. Rather it was because he had a big mouth! Peter said what he thought and that often got him into trouble. He had messed things up before when Jesus was alive, though he had been forgiven for that. However, he just couldn't be quiet and melt into a corner. Peter was Peter!

King Herod made plans to have Peter arrested during a special feast day so that more people would see what a great ruler he was. His plan was carried out. Peter was arrested and put in prison. To be absolutely sure he couldn't escape, sixteen soldiers were given the job of guarding him. Sixteen! Four soldiers were on duty at a time, and they worked six-hour shifts. Herod's plan was to have Peter tried publicly after the Passover Feast, no doubt assuming that he would be found guilty and executed. So Peter was very securely held and there was no hope of him getting out. Or was there?

That's where Rhoda comes in. She probably spent the whole evening opening and closing the outside door of Mary's house because those who were gathered there were scared and would have wanted it kept locked. They had good reason to be scared. Remember that Herod and his henchmen were out to get them. Inside there was a prayer meeting going on. Men and women, and perhaps young people as well, prayed for Peter to be released from prison.

Rhoda was probably praying herself when she heard a knock at the outside door. She went to the door right away because it wasn't safe to keep Christians standing outside longer than was necessary. The man outside spoke before she opened the door and … it couldn't be … could it? Of course it could be! It was! It was Peter! Rhoda was SO excited that God had heard and answered their prayers that she raced inside to tell everyone. The only thing was … she forgot to open the door and let Peter in!

Meanwhile, outside the door, Peter stood and knocked … and knocked.

'Peter's at the door!' Rhoda said, interrupting the prayer meeting.

'You're out of your mind,' she was told. Didn't she know that Peter was under armed guard in prison?

'But he is,' she insisted. 'Peter's at the door!'

As they were a kind bunch, they decided that it must be Peter's angel that had made Rhoda think their friend was free. Meanwhile, still outside the door, Peter stood and knocked … and knocked … and knocked … and knocked.

'There IS someone at the door,' one of the people at the prayer meeting said. 'I can hear knocking.'

At last they took Rhoda seriously. The door was opened … and there was Peter! They were astonished! Hustling Peter safely inside they all asked him questions at once.

'If you sit down quietly, I'll tell you what happened,' Peter said, and this was his story.

As they already knew, he'd had four guards looking after him. Peter, chained to his sentry, had been fast asleep. Suddenly an angel of the Lord appeared and a light shone in the cell. The angel struck Peter on the side and woke him up.

'Quick, get up!' the angel told him.

Peter was able to get up because the chains that had bound him to the soldiers had fallen off his wrists!

'Put on your clothes and sandals,' said the angel.

He did what he was told immediately.

'Wrap your cloak around you and follow me,' the angel ordered.

With his cloak tight round about him Peter followed the angel out of the prison, all the time thinking he was seeing a vision! He didn't realise that it was actually happening!

Peter and the angel passed the first set of prison guards. Then they passed the second set of prison guards. Both lots were either asleep or God kept them from seeing what was going on in front of their noses. As they came to the iron gate of the prison it swung open to let them through! They were walking along the street when suddenly Peter realised he was alone. The angel had left him … and it hadn't been a vision! He was free! Peter realised that God had sent his angel to rescue him from Herod's clutches and from those who hated the truth about Jesus. Knowing that his friends would be at Mary's house, Peter headed in that direction, knocked on the door … and you know the rest of the story!

Sometimes when we pray we forget to look for God's answers. That's a really silly thing to do if we believe that God hears and answers prayer. It's a good idea to write down important things that we pray about and then to make a note when God answers our prayers. And remember, sometimes God's answer is 'yes', sometimes his answer is 'no' and sometimes his answer is 'not yet'. It can be hard to work out the difference between 'no' and 'not yet' answers. When that happens Christians should just keep on praying.

JUST THIRTEEN

There was fear in the air; if you stretched out your hand you could almost feel it. It was AD 303 and the Emperor Diocletian was determined to get rid of all Christians in the Roman Empire. Years later, when histories were written about this time, it was called the Great Persecution. People are persecuted when they are badly treated for what they are or what they believe. And that's exactly what was happening to Christians in Rome at that time.

The Emperor came up with a plan. He knew that the God worshipped by Christians would not allow his followers to worship any other gods. Of course, there are no other gods. Anything that people worship that is not the one true God is an idol, and idols are really useless for they do not live or help or save as it is only the one true God who does that. Emperor Diocletian believed in the Roman gods. The twelve (yes twelve!) main Roman idol gods were Jupiter and Juno, Neptune and Minerva, Mars and Venus, Apollo and Diana, Vulcan and Vesta, Mercury and Ceres. But there were many, many more. People believed these gods lived on Mount Olympus (the Greeks thought their gods lived there too). And you would not believe what they got up to!

The people of the Roman Empire worshipped their gods in temples where they offered sacrifices. They also worshipped spirit gods at home and kept idols of them in their houses. It was very important to them not to offend the gods, either the main gods or the spirit gods they thought protected them and their families. Of course, when Christians refused to worship them, the people feared that their gods would be offended and start causing problems! So the ordinary people of Rome were afraid of Christians and the troubles their beliefs could cause. And fear sometimes makes people behave in very nasty ways.

Back to the Emperor's plan. He encouraged his people to fear Christians and he made a great show of passing laws to get rid of them. One truly terrible law made it illegal not to worship Roman gods. The people thought that was a great idea. If it was illegal not to worship Roman gods then Christians would have to worship them and those who lived on Mount Olympus would be pleased and not cause earthquakes, fires and volcanic eruptions to destroy them. Anyone who didn't keep the Emperor's new laws was to be put to death, often having been tortured first.

In AD 304 the Governor of Rome's son, his name was Procop, fell in love with a thirteen-year-old girl called Agnes and sent her a gift. In those days that was the first step in a man getting to know a girl that he thought he might later want to marry. The gift arrived and Agnes realised what it meant. It was followed by another gift, and then another, all of them special things that a girl would want. The problem was that Agnes was a Christian, Procop was not, and she knew from her Bible that Christians ought not to marry those who don't believe in Jesus.

Now, as well as being small for her age and rather pretty, Agnes was an honest girl and she told Procop that she couldn't marry him. She had made a promise to God that she would follow him all of her life and that she would never marry. How she must have prayed before she sent a message to the young man! Amazingly, her message has been kept down through all these hundreds of years. 'I am already promised to the Lord of the Universe. He is more splendid than the sun and the stars, and he has said he will never leave me!'

Procop went into a fury. He accused Agnes of being a Christian and reported her to his father, the Governor. Rather than having the girl tried and found guilty, the Governor spoke to Agnes. 'I will give you wonderful gifts if you'll deny God and marry my son,' he told her. Agnes, who loved the Lord Jesus so much, said that she could not do that. As she said it, she knew exactly what might happen to her. The Governor, still trying to please Procop, had her put in chains with the promise that she would be set free as soon as she worshipped the Roman gods and agreed to the marriage arrangement. Agnes was taken to prison where she prayed so much that people said her face shone with joy. Still she would not deny Jesus and marry the young man who seemed to have fallen in love with her. The Governor tried one more really nasty trick, but it didn't work either. Agnes would not change her mind.

Remember what was going on all around Procop and Agnes at this time. Christians were being reported for believing in Jesus. They were being tried and found guilty of offending the Roman gods. Roman Emperors believed they themselves were gods so Emperor Diocletian was happy (yes, actually happy) to see Christians killed – and he did watch them being killed with his very own eyes. It was a bloodthirsty time, the Great Persecution. If two Roman citizens had a serious disagreement, it was not unknown for one to accuse the other of being a Christian as a way of getting him 'legally' killed!

This was the dangerous time Agnes was living in. As trouble heaped up against Agnes, she took it all to God in prayer and trusted him to keep her from giving in and giving up. It would have been so easy for a thirteen-year-old girl to decide that she wanted to live rather than be killed.

But instead Agnes spent more and more time in prayer during her last days here on earth as she believed that she would soon see Jesus face to face in heaven. And that's what happened. Agnes was executed in AD 304, praying as she was killed.

Diocletian's Great Persecution was the worst and most terrible persecution that the young Christian church went through. Just two years after Agnes died a new Emperor was appointed who became a Christian. He was known as Constantine the Great.

Sadly, Christians are still being persecuted in some parts of the world today. There are people in prison for serving King Jesus and some are still being killed for their faith. Perhaps you could remember to pray for them that they will be like young Agnes, and keep close to God in prayer whatever troubles they go through.

OH MUM!

Monica had a problem and her problem was her son. Now, many mothers have difficult teenagers, but most don't cause their parents nearly as much grief as this one did. He was an absolute nightmare. Here are some snapshots of his activities up to the age of sixteen – and his behaviour is not to be copied!

The boy, Augustine, was born in AD 354 in North Africa. His mother was a Christian and she prayed for her son. His father believed in the Roman gods, who were just idols and could do nothing for anyone, certainly not answer their prayers. The most pleasant thing we know about young Augustine is that, as a baby, he smiled in his sleep before he smiled awake. I don't know what that says about him, but it tells me that Monica enjoyed looking at her dear little baby boy. And we only know about his sleepy smile because his mum told her son and he wrote it in a book!

The first mistake that we find Augustine making when he was quite young is that he prayed to God that he wouldn't be found out and punished for doing wrong. He didn't mind doing wrong, in fact he enjoyed it, but he didn't want his teacher to find out and punish him. So he knew about prayer and we know who taught him that. It's just a pity that he didn't pray for God to forgive him rather than let him off. Augustine's mother knew about it, mothers usually do, and she prayed.

Then there was all Augustine's naughtiness. For example, when he was a boy he used to steal food from home and alcohol from his dad's cellar. Sometimes he ate all the food himself and drank all the wine. That certainly wouldn't have done him any good. Other times he shared it with his friends and made them drunk. He was also a liar, and he enjoyed it. He felt clever and superior when he wasn't caught. But Monica knew about it. Mothers can usually recognise lies, and she prayed.

As he climbed up through his teens Augustine's behaviour went from bad to worse. When he was sixteen he finished school and spent a year at home while his dad raised money to send him away to study. You don't want to know what all he got up to that year. But Monica knew, mums normally do, and she kept praying. You see, she understood that God was so great that he could even forgive her son's sins.

Now for something that will show you just how bad Augustine's behaviour had become, and how much his mum needed to keep praying. One day, when he should have been doing something constructive, he was wandering around looking for mischief. He saw a tree heavily laden with ripe pears. Now, naughty young people might steal a few and eat them. Very naughty young people might steal a lot and sell them to make some money to get up to more mischief. But it takes a really bad person to steal all the pears off a tree and then throw them one by one into a field of pigs. Poor Monica must have wept many tears when she heard news of what he'd done. Her son seemed to be digging himself ever deeper into a hole that could land him in prison or worse, but she kept praying.

From home Augustine went to study in Carthage, a town in North Africa, and then after a time teaching he moved to Rome. In order to do that he played a really dirty trick on Monica. His dad was by then dead, and Monica was really worried about what Augustine would get up to in Rome. She had good reason to be! So she followed her son north to the Mediterranean coast where he was going to board a ship bound for Italy. The night before he was due to sail, Monica clung to him to stop him going. She wept over him. She pleaded with him to change his mind, and she prayed ... how she prayed.

Augustine was thoroughly fed up with his mother and annoyed by her tears and prayers. Giving her a time of departure, and telling her he'd see her in the morning before the ship sailed, he left and went off to bed. When Monica arrived at the given time the next morning her son's ship was already on the open sea. He had lied about the time and escaped! But it was just as well Monica was the woman she was for Augustine needed her prayers soon after he arrived in Rome. He was so ill for a while that he almost died.

It would take a whole book to tell Augustine's story and it wouldn't be a very decent book because of all he got up to. So we'll fast-forward a few years to find Augustine and his friend in a garden. They have been living in Milan with Monica who has been praying to God about her son. To Augustine's great amazement, God speaks to him in a way he just can't ignore. Augustine became a Christian. I don't think that Monica would have been amazed because she prayed knowing that God would answer. The words seem very old-fashioned, but this is what Augustine wrote after he told his mother that he'd been converted.

'Thence we go in to my mother; we tell her; she rejoiceth; we relate in order how it took place; she exulteth, and triumpheth, and Blessed God.'

Monica lived for two years after Augustine became a Christian which was just long enough to see the beginnings of how God was to use him. When Augustine's unbelieving friends saw the difference God made in his life they were amazed and had to think seriously about Christianity themselves. Not only that, when people started teaching things that were not in the Bible, and causing terrible trouble in the church, Augustine was clever enough to work out what was true and to help sort out the problems. Because he had a reputation for being exceedingly clever, people listened to what he had to say.

Monica had prayed for her son through the bad years and continued to pray for him in the good years after he became a Christian. She didn't live to see how God would ultimately use Augustine. His influence stretches down through the centuries right to the present day. And there's a lesson for us there. We know when we pray what it is we ask for. But God is able to give us more than we ask for, even more than we can think or imagine, because he is so amazingly wonderful.

TO BURMA WITH LOVE

Ann's childhood home was full of people and happy laughter. Her dad even had a ballroom built on to their home for grand occasions! Born in America in 1789, Ann lived in a wealthy family and might have expected to marry a rich man and settle down to a comfortable life with more happy laughter as their babies were born.

When she was a teenager, Ann asked Jesus to be her Saviour and that set her course for life. She prayed a prayer that God heard and answered. Ann prayed, 'Direct me in thy service, and I ask no more. I would not choose my position of work, or place of labour. Only let me know Thy will, and I will readily comply.' The language is old-fashioned, but what Ann was praying was this. She asked God to show her where to go, what to do, and how to serve him, saying that was what she wanted to do.

God heard Ann's prayer and led her to the opposite side of the world! Here is how that happened. When she was twenty-one years old she believed that the Lord was calling her to be a missionary. Now, that was quite an extraordinary thing as no missionaries had gone overseas from America ever before, and certainly no women! At the same time some young men were meeting together to pray about foreign missions. One of them, Adoniram Judson, met Ann, fell in love with her and asked her father if they could marry. Mr Hasseltine said that he couldn't take such a massive decision and that it was up to his daughter. Ann believed this was what God wanted her to do, despite the dangers that missionary work would involve. 'I dare not decline an offer I believe to be God's will,' she told her father.

Ann and Adoniram were married in 1812 and the very next day they set sail from Salem, Massachusetts for India. Six other missionaries left with them and these eight were the first Protestant missionaries to leave the shores of America to take the good news about the Lord Jesus Christ to another land. After their very long voyage the Judsons were not allowed to settle in India and moved on to Burma, where 15 million people lived who had never heard of Jesus.

Ann's prayer for Burma was this:

O thou Light of the world, dissipate (melt away) the
thick darkness which covers Burma, and let thy light

arise and shine. O display thy grace and power among the Burmese. Subdue them to thyself, and make them thy chosen people.

It would be exciting to be able to say that many men and women, boys and girls, believed in God. But the truth is that after nine years of working there only eighteen people had been converted, which works out at an average of just two a year. And it would be nice to say that Ann's Burmese home was happy and wealthy like her old home in America. But that wasn't the case. Adoniram and Ann had very little money and they had much sadness in their lives.

When they first went to Burma the Judsons wore their American clothes, but they didn't suit the climate at all and Ann looked so dull compared to her brightly dressed neighbours. Before long they decided to wear Burmese clothes to help them to fit in – and be more comfortable too. Ann worked very hard to get to know her neighbours and eventually (it took a long time) she gathered a little group of women together on Sunday afternoons. They were fascinated by the stories she told them, stories taken straight from the Bible. She also taught them to pray. Prayer was so much part of Ann's daily life that she wanted it to be part of their lives too. God was beginning to answer her prayer to let his light rise and shine in the hearts of the Burmese people.

Because Ann knew that God answers prayer, she wrote long letters to her friends back home in America telling them things about Burma that they could never have imagined and asking for their prayers. She wrote about how terribly badly women were treated, how unwanted baby girls were sometimes killed or left out to die and how very young girls were married to older men they didn't like – or even know! Of course, because the Judsons were among the very first American missionaries, all this was news to the churches. Prayer meetings sprang up and people used Ann's letters to show them what to pray for. So while Adoniram and Ann were working and praying in Burma, their friends – and thousands of others they'd never met – prayed for their work in America! God heard and answered and, little by little, Burmese people saw how differently Adoniram and Ann lived, and how differently they treated their own little daughter.

'Your religion is good for you, ours for us,' Burmese people often told the Judsons. But the truth was that the Burmese religion didn't explain that Jesus had died to save them from their sins and it didn't show them the way to heaven. So it wasn't good for them. However, over time the Burmese people did begin to hear the truth. God answered Ann's prayer to use her where he wanted, how he wanted and in whatever kind of situation he chose.

Sometimes the situations in which God chose to use the Judsons weren't comfortable, like the time

Adoniram was held in prison and Ann wasn't able to leave the safety of their house. Or when Adoniram's huge amount of work on translating the Bible into Burmese was in danger of being seized and destroyed. God gave Ann a quick mind that day and she and her helper wrapped the papers up and buried them!

Ann Judson was just thirty-seven when she died in 1826, but God continued to answer the prayers she had prayed. Adoniram remained in Burma until he died twenty-four years later. By then there were sixty-three churches in Burma with 163 Burmese church leaders. Think about that and remember Ann's prayer.

> 'O thou Light of the world, dissipate (melt away) the thick darkness which covers Burma, and let thy light arise and shine. O display thy grace and power among the Burmese. Subdue them to thyself, and make them thy chosen people.'

By 1850 God's gracious answer was that the Light of the World was melting away the thick darkness that covered Burma, and his light had arisen and was shining.

As a young woman Ann prayed for God to show her his will and she would do it. That should be every Christian's prayer ... and we have no idea how he will answer it. But he will! And when she was in Burma, Ann did a sensible thing. She let her Christian friends know what the problems were and

asked them to pray. Ann learned that in her Bible for that's what Paul did, he asked for prayer as he went on his missionary journeys.

THE SISTER WHO CARED

Amelia lived in a very busy household in Barnsley, in England's South Yorkshire. Her dad was an apothecary; we would call him a chemist or pharmacist today. That was a very responsible job as people often went to apothecaries rather than doctors because doctors cost more money. The Taylors had three children, Louisa, Hudson and Amelia, who was the youngest.

Because they lived in an apothecary's home the children were brought up hearing about people's illnesses and what herbs and drugs and treatments could help them. They were also brought up hearing about China. Mr Taylor had a special interest in China and tried to learn all he could about that faraway country.

As Amelia and her brother and sister grew up they too learned a great deal about China because their dad talked so much about it. Not only that, he prayed about it for Mr Taylor was a Christian. There can't have been many children in Barnsley who knew quite as much as Louisa, Hudson and Amelia did about such a distant land!

Today you can get to the land of China in a day by air. When Amelia was young, in the 1830s, it would have taken the best part of a year to go to China and back! So although Mr Taylor was fascinated by that country there was absolutely no question of him ever going there.

His prayer was that those who went to China would tell the people about the Lord Jesus Christ and that they would trust in him as their Saviour.

The church that the Taylor family went to was very special to them. Amelia couldn't remember when she first heard the story, but she seemed to have known it forever. Her great-grandfather, who was a stonemason, had helped cut the stones for their church and had then joined the builders as they erected the building. As Amelia sat waiting for the services to begin, she may have looked around the church and wondered which of the stones had been cut by her great-grandfather.

While Amelia was still a young girl she learned a really important lesson. She learned that the church isn't really a building at all; it is the people who are inside it worshipping God. No doubt her father explained that those who believe in Jesus are 'living stones' that make up a living church. And the Bible tells us that the most important 'stone' of all, the 'foundation stone' is the Lord Jesus Christ himself.

Hudson, who was two years older than Amelia, didn't keep very good health. It seemed that if there was a bug to be caught, he would catch it. Because of that he didn't go to school. Instead, he stayed at home and had lessons from his mother. Of course, Amelia joined in as soon as she was old enough and they were taught together. So they became really good friends. As he grew older and kept better health, Hudson went off to join the other boys at their local school. And when he left school Hudson started work in his father's business and then moved to a job in a Barnsley bank.

Much to her parents' delight, and in answer to their many, many prayers, Amelia asked Jesus to forgive her sins and be her Saviour when she was a young teenager. There was a change in Hudson's life too, but a very different one. Instead of staying at home, her brother packed his case and moved away north to Hull, where he became a medical assistant to a doctor. Amelia missed her brother very much and she prayed for him. The girl understood that Hudson knew all about Jesus but had not asked him to be his Saviour. So Amelia prayed for him to become a Christian. In fact, she was so loving and caring that she wrote a promise in her notebook. 'I will pray every day for Hudson's conversion.' Day followed day and week followed week and Amelia prayed for her brother every day for a month. Having made her decision, that faithful girl kept her promise ... and her brother knew nothing at all about it.

By then Hudson was seventeen years old and Amelia was fifteen. He came home for a visit and, being seventeen, he was bored and looking for something to do or some interesting book to read. Browsing through the books in the bookcase at home produced nothing that appealed to him. Then a little basket caught his eye. It was full of pamphlets called tracts, booklets written to tell people about Jesus.

'I know what this will be like,' he thought, as he picked up one of them. 'It will start with an interesting story and then end up with a sermon. But I'll just read the story and not bother with the sermon.'

Now, Hudson had no way of knowing what was happening about fifty miles away, where his mother was staying for a time. Later on, when they discussed dates and times, they were able to put the whole story together. What happened was this. As Hudson took the leaflet to a quiet place to read, his mum was praying for her son to believe in Jesus. She prayed and prayed, and he read ... and forgot to stop reading before the sermon! In fact, God answered Mrs Taylor's prayer just as she was praying and

Hudson suddenly realised that what he had heard about Jesus was true! He knelt down and asked God to forgive his sins and asked Jesus to be his Saviour. An extraordinary thing happened. Just at that very time, Mrs Taylor knew in her heart that her prayers had been answered. Instead of pleading with God to save Hudson, her prayer changed and she started praising him for saving her boy!

Back home in Barnsley Hudson told his sister Amelia the splendid news and she was absolutely delighted.

'Please don't tell Mum,' he said to her. 'I want to choose the right time to tell her myself.'

Two weeks later Mrs Taylor came home from her time away.

'Mother, I've such good news for you!' he said.

'I know, my boy,' his mum smiled, and gave him the biggest, tightest hug you can imagine!

'Why?' asked Hudson. 'Has Amelia broken her promise? She said she would tell no one.'

'No,' his mother assured him, 'she has not.' And she went on to explain exactly what happened. And that's when they worked out that her prayers and his conversion were at exactly the same time!

One day, some time later, Hudson picked up a notebook that he thought was his own though it actually belonged to Amelia. Opening it, he read the words she had written a month before he became a Christian. 'I will pray every day for Hudson's conversion.' Then Hudson knew that not only his parents had prayed for him, but his young sister had been praying too.

Over the years their prayers were answered in a most wonderful way. Hudson Taylor eventually went as a missionary to China. In fact, he started the largest of all missions to that great country, the China Inland Mission. CIM is now part of OMF International and continues to work in China today and also in eleven other countries in the Far East.

Amelia did the best thing she could possibly do for her brother when she prayed for him. You may have family members who are not yet Christians. The best thing you can do for them is to pray.

WE'LL COME FOR
THE JOKE!

The two young women talked quietly and seriously together.

'There really is a need for a woman leader!' Miss Francis said, smiling.

'There certainly is!' agreed Miss Baler. 'And, yes, I would like to go to Bethnal Green to see the meeting for myself. That would help me to think it through.'

That was how Miss Francis and Miss Baler came to visit the London City Mission's work in Bethnal Green. They were very warmly welcomed by the missionary, John Galt. And no words could possibly describe how glad he was to see them.

There was a Mothers' Meeting at Bethnal Green when he began his mission work there. But not long after he arrived the women who ran it left. Knowing that the poor women of Bethnal Green – and they really were poor – loved going to the meeting and were helped by it, John had decided to lead it himself until a suitable woman came along!

This was in the last year of the nineteenth century when such a thing would have been unheard of and more than a little embarrassing for John Galt. Would you like to know why? Well, as the leader, John was expected to admire all the new infants, make all the right cooing noises and help cut out cloth to make baby clothes! However, John wasn't married and he knew almost nothing about babies or baby clothes! The women who attended found it very funny. 'We'll all be here if it's only for the joke,' one told him!

Out of desperation, John borrowed books that were suitable to be read aloud to the women at the meetings, but what they really needed was a female leader. So he prayed that God would send one. And he sent two – Miss Francis and Miss Baler. Much to John Galt's huge relief they agreed to take over at Bethnal Green and then a year later Miss Baler agreed to become John's wife.

John Galt was moved by London City Mission to Poplar, a very poor area where most of the men worked as day labourers at the docks. That meant they were only employed one day at a time and paid at the end of the day. Mrs Galt felt sorry for the women who never knew from day to day if their husbands were going to find work. Most of the women worked at home doing things like making matchboxes for a criminally small amount of money. The situation in Poplar was bad all year round and worse in the winter.

It was on a freezing winter day that John came home one day with a very sorry story.

'I visited a home that nearly broke my heart,' he told his wife. 'The father who is half starved and exhausted was out looking for work. The mother was also half starved and half dressed too. She'd on hardly any clothes and the only heat she was getting was from the baby she was holding in her arms. Her two little boys were crouching down on the floor together to keep each other warm and all they had for shoes was rags wound round their feet.' Mrs Galt listened carefully. The problem was that the great River Thames had frozen over and the men had no work as there were no ships coming in. No work meant no money, no fuel and no food. It was just terrible.

'How can we help them?' the Galts asked each other. Counting out their money they found they had exactly seventy-four pence. Kneeling side by side, the couple asked God to use their money and to provide in other ways for the poor people round about. Knowing that God hears and answers the prayers of his people, they ordered fifty loaves of bread. John had counted fifty families in desperate need. Meanwhile, Mrs Galt sat down and wrote to four friends. She didn't ask them for money, rather she described the situation in

Poplar and explained that they had no more money of their own to help.

In the following morning's post two of her friends replied, enclosing seventy-five pence, almost exactly what they had spent and enough to buy another fifty loaves. But by then John had thought of a further twenty-five families in dire need. Mrs Galt and her husband discussed the matter, prayed about it and then ordered seventy-five loaves of bread. God heard and answered the Galts' prayers and the following morning the postman brought enough money to buy bread for all seventy-five families. The ice on the Thames grew thicker and there was still no work. Each day John and Mrs Galt found more starving families. And day after day God answered their prayers, providing enough money to buy them bread.

One day, nearly three weeks later, a letter came from one of the ladies who had replied on the very first day. The kind woman finished with, 'I have pleasure in enclosing double the first amount.' But she forgot to put her money in the envelope! Mrs Galt told her husband and they waited to see how God would solve the problem. And they prayed, how they prayed.

The following morning brought splendid news. There was a letter from that woman with her money plus more from her husband and son-in-law. No money at all came in after that, not a penny, but that was enough to buy bread for the starving families until the day, the exact day, when the ice on the great River Thames thawed and all the men went back to work. Just imagine the joyful prayers Mrs Galt and her husband prayed that day!

On the day when John told his wife about the poor family with their two little boys and baby, Mrs Galt didn't just pray for God to supply what was needed. She gave every last penny to buy bread for those boys and others like them. When we see people in need it is right to pray, God wants us to do that, but we also have to ask ourselves if there is any way that the Lord can use us to help them ourselves.

GOD'S ANSWER WAS 'NO'

Amy lived in a noisy house because she had six younger brothers and sisters. With their parents, Mr and Mrs Carmichael, they lived in Millisle, Northern Ireland. From a very young age Amy was full of adventure and often full of mischief. Because she was the eldest she was very much the ringleader. If there was fun to be had, Amy was there organising it. If there were mysteries to be solved, Amy was in the thick of the investigation. And if there was noise to be made, she was right in there with the noisiest of them!

The Carmichael home was a fun place to live. It was also a serious place to live because the children were taught that God saw them wherever they were and whatever they were doing. From their very earliest days Amy and her brothers and sisters heard about the Lord Jesus Christ and were encouraged to ask him to be their Saviour. Mr Carmichael took family worship, reading the Bible with his children and praying with them too. And the children also heard their mother's prayers, especially if something was upsetting them.

Amy knew that if anything was wrong, she could tell God all about it. And something was seriously wrong for Amy had brown eyes. Now, brown eyes see as well as blue and green eyes, but she thought they didn't look nearly so pretty. She had friends with blue eyes and she wanted to be like them. So, one night before she went to bed she made a decision. She would ask God to change her eyes from brown to blue and that's exactly what she did. That might seem a very strange prayer, but it was a good prayer too because it showed that she really believed that God could work miracles.

The next morning, fully expecting her prayer to be answered, Amy Carmichael looked in her mirror and found that she still had beautiful brown eyes … only she didn't think they were beautiful at all. She had prayed for something; God had answered and his answer was 'No'. If God said 'Yes' to all our prayers, he would be just like a great big heavenly slot-machine – put in your prayer and get whatever you want. Our God is much greater and more wonderful than that. He knows what is best for us and that's what he gives us. It was best for Amy to have brown eyes but it would be a long time before she would understand the reason why.

Amy was a happy girl and she lived in a happy home. But when she was twelve years old she went off to boarding school in Yorkshire, England, and she was not at all happy there. Before that she had been taught at home so it was something of a culture shock to be in school in the first place, and to be away from home made it even more difficult. However, God had plans for her time in school and it was while she was a pupil there that Amy Carmichael became a Christian. Her dad and mum must have been delighted. The Bible tells us that even the angels in heaven rejoice when someone believes in Jesus!

Years passed and God called Amy to be a missionary in Japan. She sailed there in 1893, when she was twenty-six years old. So the young brown-eyed woman went to work in a country where everyone had brown eyes. That must have helped her to fit in. The fact that God had answered 'No' to her prayer for blue eyes didn't put Amy off praying. We have a splendid example of that from her short time in Japan.

Plans were being made for Amy to visit Hirosi, a Buddhist village with only a handful of Christians. Before she went, Amy felt strongly that she should pray that one person would believe in Jesus during her visit and this is what she did. And do you know what? One person believed in Jesus! Those who worked with Amy were absolutely delighted that her prayer had been answered. The next time she was going to Hirosi, she felt very strongly that she should pray that two people would become Christians. God heard and answered her prayer and the missionaries and Japanese Christians thanked the Lord with great joy.

A fortnight later Amy was due to visit Hirosi again and this time she believed God was asking her to pray for four people to come to faith. But her fellow missionaries weren't so sure.

'That's expecting too much,' they warned her, and then promised to pray for two rather than four.

Amy wouldn't budge. She believed God was going to save four people and that's what she prayed for. Perhaps her fellow missionaries felt a little sad at their lack of faith when four people trusted in the Lord Jesus. Not only that, but they burned their Buddhist idols which was a hugely brave thing to do in a land where idols were worshipped.

From Japan Amy Carmichael moved to India in 1895 and it was there that she discovered why God had given her brown eyes in the first place, and why he hadn't changed their colour to blue in answer to her prayer. Amy lived right at the bottom tip of India in Tamil Nadu and before being there very long she took to wearing Indian dress. Her work involved travelling from village to village helping people and telling them about Jesus. Of course her Indian dress and her brown eyes made her fit into the villages because she looked very much like a local woman! Had she had fair hair and blue eyes everyone would have known she was a foreigner.

Six years later something happened that changed Amy's work. A woman brought a little girl to her for safekeeping. She was given the name Pearl Eyes. Why did she need safekeeping? Well, to understand that you have to know a truly horrible thing. At that time little girls were kept in Hindu temples to serve the priests by doing things that children ought never to do. Little Pearl (as she became known) was just five and she had already run away from the temple twice and been caught and taken back.

From then on Amy's job was clear. God had called her to save little girls from the temples, and little boys too, when she discovered they were being hurt. That was the start of her children's homes and a work that became known as the Dohnavur Fellowship. It was dangerous work because Amy was rescuing children who were being searched for as runaways! She needed to look as much like an Indian woman as possible so as not to draw attention to herself and she could only carry that off because her eyes were as brown as Indian eyes.

By the time Amy Carmichael died in 1951, after spending more than fifty years in India, there were over 900 people in the Dohnavur 'family', those who had been rescued and those who cared for them. How often she must have thanked God for not saying 'yes' to her prayer for blue eyes.

Remember Amy when God says 'No' to your prayers. God always answers what is best for us, even when we don't understand that. Sometimes we understand years later, as Amy did, but not always.

ELMA AND HER
TAPPER

Elma was an ordinary little girl brought up on the east coast of Scotland. She had no brothers or sisters; she had her mother and father all to herself. From time to time her ankles and elbows, her fingers and toes ached.

'It is just childhood arthritis,' her doctor said. 'You'll grow out of it.'

And that's exactly what seemed to happen. When Elma was thirteen years old her joints gave her no pain at all. She could run and jump, skip and swim. It was great!

By the time she was seventeen Elma could only move her right arm, and she could only move it a tiny little bit. The rest of her was stuck absolutely rigid. Elma saw several different doctors and tried different kinds of medicines, but still she couldn't move. Having always been a shy girl, now that she felt that her body was all twisted and useless she didn't want to go out and meet people at all. In any case, the only way she could go out was to have her bed carried and that was a lot of work for her parents.

As a young girl Elma had gone to Sunday School and she believed that God existed. She wasn't angry at God for making her as she was, but it did upset her that her mother had no time or energy to do anything but look after her. She sometimes prayed that God would make her better, but that didn't seem to help. For a while Elma enjoyed having pen-friends. But that became a problem as she grew up because she had to tell her mother what to write in the letters. Then when her pen-friends replied, her mother or father had to hold up their letters in front of her in order to read them. It seemed that she could have nothing private and nothing secret. And all girls have times they want to be private and things they want to keep secret.

That's when someone thought of giving Elma a tapper, a long cane with a pencil taped to the end that she could have strapped to her 'good' arm. Her dad made a frame that stood straight up and down at the end of Elma's bed and a sheet of paper was pinned to it. Then Elma moved her arm the tiny bit she could and concentrated for all she was worth. Struggling to keep the pencil end on the paper ... she managed to write E...L...M...A in big shaky letters! She could write! Elma Alexander could write to her own pen-friends. Mind you, it would take a lot of sheets of paper to make up a letter with writing that big! She practised and practised and practised until she could write smaller letters and get a fair number of words on to a big sheet of paper. For Elma that was like climbing Mount Everest!

When she was thirty-six years old, a friend asked Elma where she would go if she died that night. That really made her think. She believed God existed but she hadn't asked Jesus to be her Saviour. Over the next year Elma read the whole Bible right through and in November 1972 she became a Christian. She didn't suddenly get better. Elma wasn't miraculously able to walk or even wipe her nose or feed herself. But she did know that when she died she would go to heaven to be with Jesus. Elma learned to pray and one of the things she prayed was that God would help her not to complain about being so disabled and that she would be content to lie on her little bed all day, every day with only her tapper allowing her to do anything for herself.

After Elma Alexander's parents died, she continued to live alone. Carers came in a number of times a day. They washed her, dressed her, fed her and did everything else that needed done. For many years, Elma also had her cat Benje for company and she had her POSSUM. This possum wasn't an animal with big eyes and a long tail. It was a Patient Operated Selector Switching Unit Mechanism. You may need to read that over again! Using just her tapper to touch a computer keyboard attached to her POSSUM, Elma could use the telephone, open and close the curtains, switch on her television, radio and CD player She could also operate her computer and printer.

Picture Elma. She lay on her little bed in the living room of her home. Her head was held to the right-hand side and she couldn't turn it at all. If you visited, you had to sit at the other side to be seen. Elma wore spectacles and hearing aids because her sight and hearing were not very good. The movement in her right arm that operated her tapper was so slight that you had to watch for it to see it. Someone had to feed her from a spoon. She couldn't clean her teeth or wipe tears from her eyes. And she couldn't toilet herself or wash. Elma was totally dependent on carers to look after her.

On the east coast of Scotland where Elma lived, the mist sometimes rolls in from the sea and hangs like a fog in the air. That kind of mist is called a haar. Elma, who enjoyed writing poems, wrote about the haar.

In the haar
Before the world was massed
Before creation began
Even then my God knew me
And planned me

74

And loved me
In the Haar.

Isn't that amazing! In her poem Elma says that she can't see clearly because of the haar. She understands that God knows how disabled she is and that, for reasons that she cannot understand, he planned it that way. And she knows that God loves her, even though she doesn't understand why she is as she is.

Elma was only out of her room perhaps twice or three times a year when she would be taken – still on her little bed – in the back of someone's estate car to a meeting or concert or, believe it or not, on a short holiday! She never wrote a book or composed music. Elma didn't speak at meetings or teach Sunday School. She didn't nurse sick babies or go to India to be a missionary. To anyone who didn't know her Elma Alexander's life must have seemed truly awful.

But it wasn't! God heard and answered Elma's prayer for contentment. She was a gentle and happy lady despite everything and she just didn't know how to complain. Those who visited Elma remembered her smile rather than her disability. And those who spoke to her didn't have long to wait before she talked about how good God had been to her over the years. Elma Alexander died when she was sixty-six years old and went to heaven to meet Jesus face to face.

When Elma was young she sometimes prayed to be healed, but God said 'no' to that prayer. Years later, she prayed for contentment and everyone who knew her was aware that he answered that prayer in a very wonderful way.

THE TEACHER'S
HIGH-HEELS

When Dimitry Mustafin was at primary school in Russia in the 1950s, his country had a Communist government and Communists do not believe in God. His teachers taught that Jesus Christ was a hero of fairy tales, like Pinocchio or Little Riding Red Hood. He learned that the Bible was a collection of fairy tales, forbidden fairy tales. As a little boy Dimitry liked fairy tales and, when he asked his teacher why these fairy tales were forbidden, she answered that they were forbidden because they were written for stupid and crazy people who did not like their Motherland.

When Dimitry was a little older he had a very special teacher. Her name was Margaret Nikolaevna Zimina. She had red hair and she wore very high-heeled shoes that made little dents on the floor. Dimitry and his friends investigated the little dents and decided that they looked like tracks from a revolver! One day Dimitry discovered his teacher's story. Her mother, Teresa Markovna Zimina, had gone from Great Britain to Russia to teach English. But while she was there the Russian Revolution took place and she wasn't able to get home again. So her daughter Margaret, who was half-English, had never been to England.

Once after class Dimitry was eating with his teacher in the school's cafeteria. Margaret closed her eyes and was silent for a while. Because he realised that she was doing something that was important to her, Dimitry asked why she was silent. She told him that she was praying. He did not understand what praying was. Margaret explained that she was asking God to bless her food. When he asked her why she did that, she explained that it was because the Lord provided their food. Being a good young Communist Dimitry wanted to explain to her that it was collective farmers who provided food for them, not the Lord. But he felt that would probably hurt his teacher. That was the first time that Dimitry had met a teacher who prayed to the Lord and trusted him.

Years later, in 1985, Dimitry met teacher Margaret once again. By then he was grown up and was a university professor. They met when he was on holiday and they had plenty of time to spend talking about his schooldays. Margaret Nikolaevna Zimina told Dimitry about family members she might have in Britain although she didn't know if any of them were still alive or even existed. Dimitry felt that Margaret was very lonely and said that perhaps it was time for her to go to Britain in order to find her family. However, Margaret said that she was too old to get permission from the Soviet Government, and that she didn't have enough money anyway. Then she explained that during Communist times it was dangerous to keep in touch with people abroad. If you did that you might be accused of being a spy and put in prison.

'No, Dimitry,' she said sadly. 'I will never be able to visit my dear Great Britain. But I hope that one day you will be very rich and famous, and you will be invited to Great Britain. Then, please, do not forget to take my greetings to my dear Motherland that I will never see in my life. Dimitry, when you go to England, please go to Trafalgar Square, stroke Nelson's Column and think of me. Then, please, go to the Houses of Parliament, find Big Ben, kiss it and remember me. And then, please, Dimitry, find in London 'Marks and Spencer Department Shop' on Oxford Street and buy me a gift from England. Buy me a pair of English very high-heeled shoes. I will pray for you, Dimitry, I am always praying for you.'

In a very wonderful way God answered Margaret's prayers. Dimitry became a Christian in 1986. Human beings are so impatient. We want our prayers answered NOW! But God often has reasons for waiting, reasons that we don't understand. For reasons that only God knows he chose not to answer Margaret Nikolaevna Zimina's prayers until some time had passed.

In 1990 Communism fell and Russian people had a new kind of freedom. It was no longer against the law to read the Bible, to become a Christian or to teach children about the Lord Jesus. And it became much easier to travel abroad. As teacher Margaret had hoped, Dimitry did go to England. He went to Trafalgar Square as soon as he arrived in London, and thought of his teacher as he stroked Nelson's Column. Then he went to Big Ben, kissed the ground near it and remembered Margaret and the lessons she taught him, both of the English language and of the Lord's love. After that he went to Oxford Street and found 'Marks and Spencer Department Shop.' Dimitry searched for the shoe department and was very glad when finally he found it. But he did not buy a pair of English high-heeled shoes. By then his beloved teacher was dead. She was always a foreigner in his country, a stranger who had never seen her Motherland. But by the time Dimitry thought of her in London she was in the only home that was ever really home to her for she was at home in heaven with Jesus.

But God continued to answer her prayers even after her death. Following the fall of Communism, when it became legal to spread the good news that Jesus is Lord, Dimitry and some friends in his church took every opportunity they could to distribute New Testaments in prisons, orphanages, hospitals, schools and other places too. In the space of just six years they gave away free of charge 337,000 copies of the New Testament and through them many, many men, women and children asked the Lord Jesus to be their Saviour. The Bible says that God gives us more than we ask or think. Dimitry's teacher Margaret Nikolaevna Zimina could never, ever have imagined how absolutely wonderfully God would answer her prayers!

When we pray we really have no idea how God might answer. That was certainly true for Margaret Nikolaevna Zimina and it may be true for any one of us.

A HOT-WATER BOTTLE AND A DOLL

Meet Ruth, a ten-year-old who lived in an orphanage at a place called Nebobongo in the country that is now the Democratic Republic of Congo, right in the middle of Africa. She was a happy girl and she sang a great deal; all African children seem to do that. Nebobongo was a large mission station, the centre of Christian work for the area. There was a hospital and a separate maternity unit where babies were born. Then there was a school where Ruth and all the other orphans were taught.

Nebobongo was not like a Western village. If you need bricks to build a new house in the West, the bricks are delivered by truck. When bricks were needed in Nebobongo they were made in the brick kiln to the northwest of the village. If you need water in the West, you turn on the tap and it runs pure and clean. Nebobongo had its own water springs. Oh, and there was a football pitch. The nurses in the hospital were all boys and young men and they loved football!

The mission at Nebobongo was very remote, right in the middle of the Congolese jungle. You would think it would be a quiet place being so far from a city. Far from it! The truth is that it was a busy bustling place and there was always plenty for Ruth and her friends to see and do. People came and went to the hospital. Dr Helen Roseveare (she was from England and white skinned) went to the orphanage every day at lunchtime to pray with the children. Ruth often saw her driving out of Nebobongo to see someone who was ill or to do hospital business in the faraway city.

One day Mama Luka (that was Dr Roseveare's Congolese name) came to the orphanage as usual. Mama Luka said that she had something to tell them before they prayed together and this was what it was.

'During the night,' said Mama Luka, 'I was called out to the maternity unit where a woman was having a baby and things weren't going well. We did everything we could to help her, but the poor woman died. The baby survived and he has a big sister, who is just two years old.'

The children listened to what Mama Luka said, sad at the thought of the woman who died.

The doctor continued. 'When the tiny baby boy was born I asked the nurse to go for the incubator to keep the infant safe and warm.'

You may know about incubators – high-tech sterile plastic hospital beds for babies with oxygen available and all kinds of other medical bits and pieces attached. The Nebobongo incubator wasn't like that. It was just a lid-less wooden box that kept the draught off! Babies were wrapped in cotton wool and put in the box with a warm hot-water bottle on either side to keep them from getting chilled.

'You know how cold it gets here at night,' Mama Luka reminded the children. 'And tiny babies need to be kept warm.'

All the children knew about the cold. It can be really hot during the day in the Congo, but it is shivery cold if you wake up during the night. They listened carefully for what was to come.

'When the nurse came back with the incubator she had really bad news. The last hot-water bottle had burst! I explained to her that the baby needed to be kept warm or it would die and that she would have to cuddle him to keep him alive.'

Was the baby still alive? the children wondered.

'When I went to the maternity unit this morning the nurse had done a good job and the little boy was still alive,' she told the orphans, 'but his big sister was crying because she was missing her mummy so much.'

85

Having told the whole story, Mama Luka prayed with the orphans. Ruth, who knew that God hears and answers prayer, came out to the front to pray.

'God,' Ruth said, 'please send a hot-water bottle so that this little baby doesn't die. God, it will be no use sending it tomorrow because we need it today. And, God, while you're at it, will you send a dolly for the baby's sister who is crying because her mummy has died.'

When people say 'Amen' at the end of a prayer, they are agreeing that God can do it. Mama Luka, the missionary, didn't say 'Amen' because she didn't think that God could possibly send a hot-water bottle and a dolly to the middle of the jungle that afternoon. It just couldn't be done!

Later that day, when Mama Luka was in the hospital ward, a man came in with a message.

'A truck has just driven in with a parcel for you. The man dropped the parcel and drove away again.'

Such a thing was unheard of in Nebobongo!

Mama Luka went out and looked at the parcel. It was wrapped in brown paper and string. The postage stamps showed it had been sent from England. It was the first parcel that she'd received in all the time she'd been in the Congo! Taking it over to the orphan home, Mama Luka brought out the children and sat them down in front of her where they could watch it being opened.

When the string was untied and the paper unwrapped, the orphans' eyes were wide open to see what was inside. There were baby clothes, bandages, soap … and then, when Mama Luka pushed her hand down inside, she felt what could only be … a … hot … water … bottle!!!

Ruth jumped to her feet and ran out to the front.

'If God sent the hot-water bottle, he'll have sent the dolly too!' she yelled delightedly.

Hauling this, that and the next thing from the parcel, Ruth reached the bottom and there, as she knew it would be, was a dolly for the baby's big sister! There was such a shout of delight as the orphans thanked God as noisily as only children can. How God must enjoy that kind of thanks!

That's a wonderful story, but that's not the end. The package had taken months to go from England to the Congo and God had it arrive there on the very day it was needed. Many months before that he had moved the hearts of some kind people thousands of miles away to pack exactly what God knew was needed to save the life of a tiny newborn boy and to comfort his sad big sister.

God doesn't just answer adult's prayers. He hears and answers the prayers of every single person who trusts in him, no matter how young they are (or how old!).

KESENE SEES IN HER HEART

You are about to meet a very special person. Her name is Kesene and she lives in Kenya. Before you meet her, you have to meet three other people, learn about a disease and discover some facts about a disability. Phew!

First of all, the people. Lorna Eglin and Betty Allcock from South Africa were missionaries at a place called Kajiado in Kenya. Georgie Orme was brought up in Scotland and joined them there. She was a missionary nurse. People who go abroad as missionaries do all kinds of jobs. They teach, nurse, preach, build houses and churches, work in orphanages and offices. A few even fly planes! But whatever else missionaries do, their main concern is to tell people about the Lord Jesus Christ. Lorna, Betty and Georgie worked together at a Child Care Centre where disabled boys and girls stayed while they learned to walk. And, of course, they taught the children about the Lord.

The disease. Polio used to be common in many countries of the world. Today children in developed countries are vaccinated against the disease and don't catch it. Often the vaccine is given on a sugar cube! Those who caught polio (mostly children) were very ill; their muscles wouldn't work and parts of their bodies became paralysed. The people worst affected couldn't even breathe and had to be put into machines known as 'iron lungs' that breathed for them until they could breathe for themselves again. Some people did get better but many were left very disabled.

The disability. This has such a big name that I'm going to break it up into little bits to make it easier to read. It's called arth-ro-gry-posis. The best way to imagine what it's like having arth-ro-gry-posis is to do an experiment. Ready? Stand up and then bend your knees tightly so that you are crouching down on the floor. Next bend your arms at the elbow. Now try walking without unbending anything and you'll find that the best you can do is a waddle. If you had arth-ro-gry-posis you could be like that all of the time. You can't catch arth-ro-gry-posis; it is something you are born with and that doesn't get better.

Now you can meet Kesene. Lorna and Betty heard about this very disabled girl and went to visit her home. Kesene was a very happy and very much loved Maasai girl. When her parents heard about the Child Care Centre they thought that their daughter might be helped there and they agreed to allow her to go. The missionaries hoped they might be able to have something done that would allow the girl to straighten up and walk more normally.

That's how Kesene came to be in Kajiado in the 1980s along with a number of boys and girls who were disabled through having had polio. The other children were able to be helped by physiotherapy, exercises and having calipers made for their thin damaged legs. Their calipers fitted into shoes – the first shoes they had ever worn. Their shoes needed to be kept in really good condition for them to support their weak ankles. Children looked after their shoes and cleaned them to keep the leather in good condition.

There is something else you have to learn about Kesene. She was blind, Kesene was born with no eyes. Having felt her friends' shoes, heard them being brushed clean, and knowing how proud the boys and girls were of them, Kesene really, really wanted a pair of her own. But things didn't work out as was hoped. Even very clever doctors couldn't help Kesene. She couldn't even wear shoes because, in a strange way, Kesene's bare feet were her eyes. She knew when she was walking on sand because she could feel it tickling between her toes. The soles of her feet complained if she was on sharp stoney ground. And if she was accidentally walking too near water, she knew because her feet felt wet.

Because Kesene was such a happy and out-going girl she had no problem at all making friends with the children she met at Kajiado. One of them sometimes acted as Kesene's eyes and here is how she did it. She walked with calipers and crutches because she had suffered from polio. Kesene waddled behind her, holding her friend by the waist, knowing that she could see where they were going!

There was a Kenyan house-mother in the Child Care Centre who loved Jesus very much. Ng'oto Samuel prayed with all the children, including Kesene. Kesene eventually believed in Jesus. Like many Africans, she just loved singing and she made up songs of her own. Here is one of them.

> I know in my heart you are a good God;
> You made Turere's toes straight because you are a good God.
> You made Nchaa's back strong because you are a good God.
> You healed Naishorua because you are a good God.

That's just one verse of the song. Kesene added verse after verse, with one line about each of the children in the Centre!

Not only was Kesene a singer, she was also a missionary. A visitor came to the Child Care Centre and Georgie was showing him around. She took him to see where the calipers were made, where the children did their physiotherapy and the special pool they exercised in. Georgie didn't tell the visitor about Jesus because she didn't want to seem to be pushing her faith on him. But Kesene was having none of that. She tugged Georgie's skirt (remember, she was crouched down all of the time) and said to the missionary in her own language, 'Ask him if he loves Jesus.' The visitor wanted to know what Kesene had said and Georgie had to tell him. That really made him think!

On Sundays the missionaries took a number of the children out to local villages to hold services. Children took part in the services. One day Kesene wanted to speak and this is what she said. 'Until I came to the Child Care Centre I didn't know that God had a son called Jesus or that he loves children. Now I know him, and I know he loves me. I don't have eyes in my body, but in my heart I see Jesus!'

Remember what missionaries do? They nurse and teach and drive and even fly, but most of all they pray that people will come to know Jesus as their Saviour. Do you think that Lorna, Betty and Georgie's prayers for Kesene were answered? What was most important for Kesene was that Jesus loved her and she knew and loved him. Is that the most important thing in your life too?

God hears every prayer and answers each one. Sometimes God's answer is 'no', sometimes it's 'yes' and sometimes it's 'not yet'. Whatever God's answer is, it's the right one for he only does what is good. All the people in this book either prayed or were prayed for. Do you pray? If you do, remember to look for answers and to thank God for them. If you don't yet pray, God is waiting to hear from you. And remember, the only way to learn to pray … is to pray!

BOOKS BY IRENE HOWAT

ON FIRE

Each of these stories is about fire – but there's not a matchstick or a marshmallow in sight! They are all from the Bible and show how God has used fire throughout scripture in a variety of ways. He used fire to get Moses to pay attention. He used it to help the Israelites find their way through the dark. He used it to keep Adam and Eve out of the garden. But fire also appears in the New Testament... soldiers with torches arrest Jesus in the garden of Gethsemane. Peter warms himself by some flames while at the same time he denies the Lord Jesus. Jesus himself cooks a fish Barbie on the beach after his resurrection and the Holy Spirit comes down on the disciples at Pentecost with tongues of flame.

ISBN: 978-1-84550-780-0

BOOKS ABLAZE

There are some bonfires in this book. Books were amongst some of the things set alight during church history. In fact flames were used to persecute Christians throughout church history. Their possessions and homes were set alight. Christians were even killed and burned for their faith. But there was one fire that didn't happen - on the 5th of November, 1605 Guy Fawkes and others decided to set fire to the Houses of Parliament in the United Kingdom. Irene Howat tells the Christian story behind this and other incidents in history. You will see how not even fire or the plans of evil men can separate Christians from the love of God.

ISBN: 978-1-84550-781-7